Strengthening the Nuclear Nonproliferation Regime

COUNCIL *on*
FOREIGN
RELATIONS

International Institutions and
Global Governance Program

Council Special Report No. 54
April 2010

Paul Lettow

Strengthening the Nuclear Nonproliferation Regime

The Council on Foreign Relations is an independent, nonpartisan membership organization, think tank, and publisher dedicated to being a resource for its members, government officials, business executives, journalists, educators and students, civic and religious leaders, and other interested citizens in order to help them better understand the world and the foreign policy choices facing the United States and other countries. Founded in 1921, the Council carries out its mission by maintaining a diverse membership, with special programs to promote interest and develop expertise in the next generation of foreign policy leaders; convening meetings at its headquarters in New York and in Washington, DC, and other cities where senior government officials, members of Congress, global leaders, and prominent thinkers come together with Council members to discuss and debate major international issues; supporting a Studies Program that fosters independent research, enabling Council scholars to produce articles, reports, and books and hold roundtables that analyze foreign policy issues and make concrete policy recommendations; publishing *Foreign Affairs*, the preeminent journal on international affairs and U.S. foreign policy; sponsoring Independent Task Forces that produce reports with both findings and policy prescriptions on the most important foreign policy topics; and providing up-to-date information and analysis about world events and American foreign policy on its website, CFR.org.

The Council on Foreign Relations takes no institutional positions on policy issues and has no affiliation with the U.S. government. All statements of fact and expressions of opinion contained in its publications are the sole responsibility of the author or authors.

Council Special Reports (CSRs) are concise policy briefs, produced to provide a rapid response to a developing crisis or contribute to the public's understanding of current policy dilemmas. CSRs are written by individual authors—who may be CFR fellows or acknowledged experts from outside the institution—in consultation with an advisory committee, and are intended to take sixty days from inception to publication. The committee serves as a sounding board and provides feedback on a draft report. It usually meets twice—once before a draft is written and once again when there is a draft for review; however, advisory committee members, unlike Task Force members, are not asked to sign off on the report or to otherwise endorse it. Once published, CSRs are posted on www.cfr.org.

For further information about CFR or this Special Report, please write to the Council on Foreign Relations, 58 East 68th Street, New York, NY 10065, or call the Communications office at 212.434.9888. Visit our website, www.cfr.org.

To submit a letter in response to a Council Special Report for publication on our website, CFR.org, you may send an email to CSReditor@cfr.org. Alternatively, letters may be mailed to us at: Publications Department, Council on Foreign Relations, 58 East 68th Street, New York, NY 10065. Letters should include the writer's name, postal address, and daytime phone number. Letters may be edited for length and clarity, and may be published online. Please do not send attachments. All letters become the property of the Council on Foreign Relations and will not be returned. We regret that, owing to the volume of correspondence, we cannot respond to every letter.

Contents

Foreword

Nuclear technology has long been recognized as capable of both tremendous benefits and tremendous destruction. With this in mind, countries have devised international arrangements intended to promote peaceful nuclear applications while preventing the spread of materials, equipment, and technologies useful for producing nuclear weapons. Today, however, it is clear that this global nonproliferation regime is falling short. North Korea withdrew from the Nuclear Nonproliferation Treaty (NPT) in 2003 and has since tested two nuclear devices. Iran, while still a party to the NPT, has developed the capacity to enrich significant amounts of uranium; many believe it is seeking to build nuclear weapons or at least attain the ability to do so. In addition, there is the challenge of facilitating the expansion of nuclear energy, something that could help reduce carbon emissions, while preventing countries from using related technologies for military purposes. Finally, the prevalence of nuclear materials only intensifies the fear that terrorist groups could acquire them through theft or a deliberate transfer from a state.

Given these challenges, it is fitting that nuclear issues are near the top of today's foreign policy agenda. President Barack Obama organized a nuclear security summit in April to discuss ways to secure nuclear materials and reduce the threat of terrorism, and NPT signatories will gather in May for the five-yearly NPT review conference. The United States and Russia have reached a successor agreement calling for further reductions in their nuclear arsenals. And the United States and others continue to pursue both sanctions and negotiations with the aim of limiting Iran's nuclear capabilities.

In this Council Special Report, Paul Lettow examines the shortcomings of the nonproliferation regime and proposes a comprehensive agenda to shore it up. He first explores the challenges facing current arrangements, chief among them the spread of enrichment and reprocessing technologies needed to produce fissile material. Lettow then makes a variety of recommendations. First, he calls for tighter sanctions on Iran with the goal of dissuading it from continuing its nuclear advances and discouraging others from following Tehran's path. To combat the spread of enrichment and reprocessing, the report urges the United States to lead nuclear suppliers in developing a system that would allow the sale of relevant equipment and technology only to countries that meet demanding criteria. As regards a potential multilateral nuclear fuel bank, the report argues for limiting participation to states that have a strong nonproliferation record and agree not to make their own nuclear fuel. Lettow further recommends a larger budget, more authority, and various policy changes for the International Atomic Energy Agency so that it can better detect dangerous violations of nonproliferation agreements. Finally, he urges a series of steps in the United Nations Security Council to punish violators and deal with countries that seek to withdraw from the NPT while in noncompliance with their obligations.

Strengthening the Nuclear Nonproliferation Regime provides an authoritative look at today's nuclear-related concerns and what can be done to address them. With its thoughtful analysis and comprehensive recommendations, it makes a strong contribution on a subject of vital importance. And given the challenges now testing the nonproliferation regime, as well as the issue's prominence in the foreign policy debate, the report could not come at a better time.

Richard N. Haass
President
Council on Foreign Relations
April 2010

Acknowledgments

The members of the advisory committee, as well as Franklin Miller and Mitchell Reiss, took time to provide expertise and insights. Many of them reviewed and commented on multiple drafts. I am deeply grateful to each of them.

CFR President Richard N. Haass, Senior Vice President and Director of Studies James M. Lindsay, and Vice President of the Washington Program Kay King made this work possible. I owe them thanks for their support and suggestions. CFR's International Institutions and Global Governance program, headed by Senior Fellow and Director Stewart M. Patrick and Deputy Director Kaysie Brown, oversaw the project from start to finish. Senior Fellow Daniel Markey provided useful comments. CFR's Editorial Director Patricia Dorff and Production Editor Lia C. Norton, along with Communications Associate Director Leigh-Ann Krapf Hess and Communications Coordinator Sarah Doolin, gave expert help.

I am indebted to Robert Nelson and Daniel Simons for their adroit research assistance. Thanks are also due to Michelle Smith.

This publication is part of CFR's International Institutions and Global Governance program and has been made possible by the generous support of the Robina Foundation.

Paul Lettow

Acronyms

CTBT	Comprehensive Test Ban Treaty
EU	European Union
FMCT	Fissile Material Cutoff Treaty
G8	Group of Eight
IAEA	International Atomic Energy Agency
NIC	National Intelligence Council
NPT	Nuclear Nonproliferation Treaty
NSG	Nuclear Suppliers Group
PSI	Proliferation Security Initiative
START	Strategic Arms Reduction Treaty
WMD	weapons of mass destruction

Council Special Report

Introduction

The international nuclear nonproliferation regime—the principal objective of which is to prevent the spread of nuclear weapons—is under severe strain. The North Korean and Iranian nuclear programs have exploited and underscored weaknesses in the regime that must be fixed if it is to serve its purpose. Those weaknesses are both structural—ambiguities and limitations in the current rules—and result from a failure to enforce the rules that exist.

The rules as currently applied have been unable to prevent the spread of enrichment and reprocessing, which can produce fuel for nuclear reactors or the fissile material for a nuclear weapon, to countries with unclear or military intentions.[1] The existing means of detecting, determining, and enforcing violations of the nonproliferation regime have proven insufficient in the face of countries determined to pursue a nuclear weapon capability. The spread of nuclear energy is opening new pathways to proliferation. And political wrangling over nuclear disarmament has too often stood in the way of progress on reforming the international system designed to prevent nuclear proliferation.

North Korea became the first state to withdraw from the Nuclear Nonproliferation Treaty (NPT) and test nuclear devices: the first outright failure of the nuclear nonproliferation regime and an ominous development. Iran, though still a nominal party to the NPT, has long been in violation of its nonproliferation obligations during its quest to become a nuclear power. The North Korean and Iranian programs have demonstrated that the regime is flawed and not being enforced adequately. At the same time, they have generated pressure on rivals to look to offsetting capabilities. They may also lead some to perceive that nuclear weapons can provide status and bargaining leverage. The confluence of those factors, unless changed, could signal the demise of the NPT regime as an effective barrier to new nuclear weapons–capable states.[2]

A world in which many countries have nuclear weapons, or latent nuclear weapon capabilities, would be disastrous for U.S. and international security. It would make nuclear terrorism more likely, embolden disruptive states that are or may become hostile to the United States, increase tensions, destabilize regional security—thus implicating the security and economic concerns of the United States—and raise the specter of innumerable routes to catastrophic conflict, especially in the Middle East and Asia.

The year 2010 presents both unprecedented challenges to the United States' enduring nonproliferation objectives and unusual opportunities to advance a compelling agenda in light of the obvious necessity to shore up the nonproliferation regime. The first half of the year encompasses two high-profile international forums for discussion of nuclear nonproliferation issues: President Barack Obama hosts a nuclear security summit in April, and the quinquennial NPT Review Conference takes place in May.

In developing its nonproliferation agenda, the Obama administration should focus on several multilateral measures. The United States should pursue meaningful sanctions against Iran—globally through the UN Security Council, if possible, and also with the European Union (EU) and other partners—to raise the costs of Iran's nuclear program and discourage others from following the same course. It should restrict the spread of enrichment and reprocessing by pushing for adoption by the Nuclear Suppliers Group (NSG) of a criteria-based approach to trade in those areas. The United States should lead an initiative to require binding adherence to the Additional Protocol, which allows inspectors some expanded access to information and sites, especially as a condition for receiving any nuclear supply. It should seek expanded inspection authorities and funds for the International Atomic Energy Agency (IAEA), spur the agency to make full use of its existing authorities and technologies, and encourage it to revise its outdated operational goals. To bolster the IAEA board of governors' ability and will to find countries in noncompliance with their nonproliferation obligations, the United States must encourage the board to set out and follow strict and objective guidelines for making that determination. And to help promote effective and expeditious enforcement of the rules of the regime—a critical weakness in the last two decades—the United States should ask the UN Security Council to set out a generic series of punitive steps that would presumptively apply to any state in breach of its nonproliferation obligations.

The United States can help address the problem of withdrawal from the NPT by promoting a UN Security Council resolution spelling out serious and automatic consequences for withdrawal from the treaty while in noncompliance, and seeking to lengthen the notice period before withdrawal.

If implemented, those measures would reinforce the basic norm of nonproliferation: that the spread of nuclear weapons is contrary to the interest of all nations, especially those without nuclear weapons. They would strengthen the nonproliferation rules and the detection and enforcement of violations and would help deter states that do not subscribe to the basic norm from pursuing their nuclear ambitions.

Background

ORIGINS AND PRINCIPLES
OF THE NONPROLIFERATION REGIME

The international nuclear nonproliferation regime comprises the Nuclear Nonproliferation Treaty; the International Atomic Energy Agency safeguards system; export control arrangements, such as the Nuclear Suppliers Group; UN Security Council resolutions; multilateral and bilateral initiatives, including the Proliferation Security Initiative (PSI); and bilateral nuclear cooperation agreements between supplier and purchaser states. It is supported by a broad range of alliances and security assurances.

The NPT is the cornerstone of the regime. It originated in the growing awareness during the 1950s and 1960s that the proliferation of nuclear weapons was inherently dangerous and served the security interests of nuclear weapon states and nonnuclear weapon states to prevent their further spread. After several years of negotiation, the NPT opened for signature in 1968 and entered into force in 1970.

Nuclear weapon states party to the treaty agree in Article I not to transfer nuclear weapons to any recipient, nor to assist, directly or indirectly, the development of nuclear weapons by others. The nonnuclear weapon states agree in Article II not to acquire nuclear weapons or seek their manufacture. Each nonnuclear weapon state further agrees in Article III to accept safeguards, via a separate agreement with the IAEA, to verify the fulfillment of its nonproliferation obligations. Article IV contains provisions on peaceful nuclear energy. It refers to an "inalienable right of all the Parties to the Treaty to develop research, production and use of nuclear energy for peaceful purposes and *in conformity with articles I and II of this Treaty*" (emphasis added).[3] In Article VI, each party to the treaty "undertakes to pursue negotiations in good faith on effective measures relating to cessation of the nuclear arms race at an early date and to nuclear disarmament, and on a treaty on general and complete disarmament under strict and effective international control." The NPT also contains a withdrawal provision, in Article X, by which a party to the treaty may withdraw with three months' notice.[4]

The five original nuclear weapon powers—the United States, the Soviet Union (Russia), the United Kingdom, France, and China—are parties to the NPT and are the only states allowed under the treaty to develop, otherwise acquire, or possess nuclear weapons. Three states—India, Israel, and Pakistan—never signed the NPT, and each is nuclear-armed. (Israel has never confirmed the existence of its nuclear weapons.) In the forty-year existence of the treaty, no state had signed it as a nonnuclear weapon state and subsequently developed nuclear weapons until North Korea did so, withdrawing from the treaty in 2003 and testing nuclear devices in 2006 and 2009.

ROLE OF THE REGIME

The nuclear nonproliferation regime has played an important role in slowing the spread of nuclear weapons and thus in furthering international and U.S. security. Within twenty years of the United States' development of the atomic bomb in 1945, the Soviet Union, the United Kingdom, France, and China had tested nuclear weapons. The number seemed poised to grow considerably. In the early 1960s, President John F. Kennedy predicted that a decade later, fifteen to twenty states would possess nuclear weapons. Yet today the total number of states that possess a nuclear arsenal stands at nine: half the number Kennedy predicted would exist by the early 1970s.

During the NPT's existence, there have been some significant nonproliferation successes. The first Gulf War and the ensuing UN Security Council–mandated inspections and sanctions regime effectively degraded the covert nuclear program in Saddam Hussein's Iraq, the magnitude of which (including work on three different enrichment technologies and some reprocessing) was startling and revelatory.[5] Belarus, Kazakhstan, and Ukraine, inheritors of nuclear weapons after the collapse of the Soviet Union, agreed to have those weapons destroyed, and joined the NPT. During its last years, the apartheid government in South Africa destroyed its covertly developed nuclear arsenal and joined the NPT. In late 2003, on the heels of the U.S.-led invasion of Iraq and the interdiction of a shipment of thousands of centrifuge parts, Libya agreed to dismantle its covert weapons of mass destruction (WMD) programs, which included a nuclear weapons program, and to begin its gradual reintegration into the international community.[6] Beyond these examples, many countries have possessed for decades the financial and technical resources to develop nuclear weapons but have refrained, although some did so after seriously contemplating or even beginning weapons programs.

The causes underlying each country's decision not to pursue nuclear weapons, to abandon weapons or weapons programs, or to be effectively stripped of them are diverse. They include the nuclear restraint imposed and enforced by the United States and Soviet Union during the Cold War, direct or threatened intervention, political transformation, and the extended deterrence provided by the U.S. nuclear arsenal.

The international nonproliferation regime has also been an integral factor. It reinforces the widely shared norm that the further spread of nuclear weapons harms the security of all nations and establishes legally binding rules. It provides basic means for other states to seek assurances that the rules are being obeyed, through IAEA safeguards, and it encompasses formal and informal mechanisms to prevent the spread of dangerous technologies, including through UN Security Council mandates and informal export control groups. It also allows for the possibility of multilateral action against violators of the regime. Preventing nations from exploiting the regime's ambiguities and flaws, cheating, or defecting from it is imperative to ensuring its continued effectiveness and U.S. national security.

Weaknesses and Challenges

In the forty years since the NPT entered into force, a number of innovations have added meaningfully to the nuclear nonproliferation regime. They include the Nuclear Suppliers Group—an informal group of nuclear-exporting countries founded in 1974 to coordinate limitations on trade in potentially dangerous nuclear-related areas—and the Proliferation Security Initiative, a voluntary, non-treaty-based group established by U.S. leadership in 2003 that aims to prevent and intercept the transfer or transit of sensitive materials and technologies to and from states and nonstate actors of proliferation concern. Nevertheless, the regime suffers from gaps and weaknesses that are increasingly evident and consequential, and from the inability or unwillingness of many states to enforce existing rules.

THE SPREAD OF ENRICHMENT AND REPROCESSING

From the advent of the atomic bomb, U.S. officials identified enormous proliferation risks inherent in the spread of enrichment and reprocessing. It was understood then, and remains true today, that the production of fissile material is the most costly, complicated, and difficult aspect of making a nuclear weapon.[7] Enrichment and reprocessing are difficult to detect, and thus are conducive to clandestine programs. In addition, some states party to the treaty have argued that the broad terms of Article IV allow, or at least do not prevent, declared enrichment and reprocessing.

Those dangers have emerged today as major threats to the viability of the nonproliferation regime. Several states have pursued clandestine enrichment or reprocessing programs, typically with help from Pakistan's Abdul Qadeer (A. Q.) Khan, who stole designs for centrifuge enrichment while working for an enrichment consortium in Europe in the 1970s, took them to Pakistan to develop the material for Pakistan's nuclear bomb, and built an international black market network that sold plans and equipment to Iran, Libya, and North Korea.

North Korea, after developing a program to reprocess spent nuclear fuel—which allowed it to produce the fissile material for a nuclear weapon—withdrew from the NPT in 2003 and tested nuclear devices.[8] Likewise, Iran, through duplicity, diplomatic stalling, and the unwillingness of its international protectors to take meaningful action to enforce the NPT regime, has been enriching uranium, the other principal method for making the fissile material for a nuclear weapon. It has done so, first covertly and now overtly, despite being in violation of its nonproliferation obligations and in defiance of several UN Security Council resolutions. The revelation in September 2009 of at least one additional covert enrichment site in Iran—located underground on an Iranian Revolutionary Guard Corps base and designed on a scale that cannot plausibly be meant to produce fuel for a nuclear power reactor but could be used to produce the fissile material for a nuclear weapon—provides further evidence of Iran's intentions and growing capabilities.[9] Iran could produce the fissile material for a nuclear weapon in short order, perhaps within a year or even six months.[10] Notably, North Korea and Iran have pursued their ambitions through the same basic route: enrichment or reprocessing on their own soil.

The North Korean and Iranian programs and the potential for further proliferation—particularly in the Middle East, as countries proceed with nuclear energy programs and leave open future options for developing a weapon—have underscored the dangers of enrichment and reprocessing. Mohammed ElBaradei, whose tenure as director general of the IAEA ended in November 2009, stated that the development of enrichment or reprocessing capabilities by individual states makes them "latent" nuclear weapon states and is "too dangerous."[11]

It is increasingly likely that countries will develop enrichment or reprocessing capabilities openly as an element of a declared peaceful nuclear program—that is, to produce nuclear reactor fuel. Under IAEA safeguards, they could thereby become latent nuclear weapon states. Another significant concern is that additional states will pursue clandestine enrichment or reprocessing, with help from other states or nonstate actors. They could also use a civil program as cover for a simultaneous, undeclared enrichment or reprocessing effort. If nonnuclear weapon states develop nuclear arsenals by technologies acquired and mastered legally as part of or masked by a peaceful nuclear program under NPT's Article IV, it would undermine the regime.

Several countries have expressed interest in, or are moving toward, new enrichment programs. For example, some countries that are significant sources of natural uranium, such as South Africa, are interested in undertaking enrichment, or at least leaving options open to enrich. Most of those countries are highly unlikely ever to develop nuclear weapons. Yet their interest in developing potentially dangerous capabilities makes it difficult to generate agreement on means to restrict the spread of enrichment and reprocessing. The danger lies in intentions, and thus requires a way either to curtail entirely the spread of the technologies or to prevent their spread to those whose aims are suspect or unclear.

A number of governments, outside experts, and nongovernmental organizations have established plans for international fuel assurances or international enrichment and reprocessing facilities to prevent the proliferation of those technologies. Yet, absent restrictive measures, countries could opt out of such initiatives at the outset, enrich and reprocess while participating, or take part initially and then withdraw. An effective strategy would combine measures to restrict the spread of these inherently dangerous technologies with fuel supply assurances or international facilities.

NONCOMPLIANCE AND ENFORCEMENT

As the cases of North Korea, Iran, and Syria—the last of which built a clandestine reactor with North Korean help that was capable of producing plutonium but was ultimately destroyed by Israeli airstrike in 2007—make clear, the existing means of detecting, determining, and enforcing violations of safeguards obligations, and the will to do so, are inadequate for the task.[12] For example, it took four years from the public disclosure by an Iranian dissident group in 2002 of Iran's initial clandestine enrichment program for the UN Security Council to act, exposing the deep flaws in the nonproliferation regime that allow the country in question to conceal and obstruct, and its defenders in the IAEA and UN Security Council to stall and impede, a noncompliance finding and meaningful enforcement. Since the Security Council first took action with respect to Iran in 2006, it has passed resolutions with considerable difficulty, imposing sanctions in only three of five resolutions.[13] Iran has defied the important demands of the resolutions. Rather than ceasing enrichment, it has expanded its program, including enrichment up to 20 percent, well beyond the level of low-enriched uranium; it refuses to implement the Additional Protocol or provide information on or access to certain critical facilities and programs; and a recent report by the new IAEA director general, Yukiya Amano, stated that Iranian programs aimed at the development of nuclear explosives "seem to have continued beyond 2004."[14] Iran is defying both the rules of the international nonproliferation regime and the efforts thus far to enforce them, which have imposed insufficient consequences. There were no UN Security Council resolutions aimed at Iran's nuclear program in 2009 or in the first three months of 2010, despite the passing of two deadlines set by the United States and the disclosure of the additional clandestine enrichment site. The processes of detection and enforcement must be made credible and effective, which means expeditious, for the regime to endure. The IAEA's ability and initiative to detect noncompliance must be bolstered, and the process by which the IAEA finds a country in noncompliance with its safeguards obligations must be reasonably timely and objective.[15] Once a party to the NPT is found in violation of its nonproliferation obligations, enforcement must follow quickly and with clear consequences.

REGIONAL PROLIFERATION CONCERNS

Nuclear proliferation endangers regional and international security in a compounding way: as additional states develop nuclear weapons capability, the more others feel their interests threatened and pressured to develop offsetting offensive (and defensive) capabilities. Thus far, North Korea's nuclear program has not prompted Japan and South Korea, which have strong security relationships with the United States, to pursue nuclear weapons of their own. That may change if North Korea retains or expands its arsenal or becomes increasingly belligerent, especially if it does so while China continues to expand its nuclear forces.

The dynamic is different in the Middle East. The U.S. National Intelligence Council (NIC) judged in 2008 that "a few of Iran's neighbors will see Iran's development of nuclear weapons or a latent weapons capability as an existential threat or as resulting in an unacceptable, fundamental shift of power in the region, and therefore will seek offsetting capabilities."[16] That trend is probably already under way. Pointing to Turkey, the United Arab Emirates, Bahrain, Saudi Arabia, Egypt, and Libya, countries that are building or have expressed interest in nuclear power facilities—despite, in most cases, possessing extensive oil and gas resources—the NIC stated that "Iran's growing nuclear capabilities are already partly responsible for the surge of interest in nuclear energy in the Middle East, fueling concern about the potential for a nuclear arms race."[17] It could take several years, perhaps ten, for any of those states to develop nuclear weapons starting from their current capabilities.[18] The most likely outcome in the event of continued Iranian progress in enrichment would be a drawn-out, rolling proliferation in the region, in which some countries follow a step or two behind Iran, first building nuclear power reactors while keeping options open for enrichment or reprocessing, and then moving to enrichment or reprocessing while keeping options open for nuclear weapons. The potential for regional instability, miscalculation, and conflict resulting in the Middle East— rather than any kind of deterrence, which was tenuous even between the United States and USSR during the Cold War—is considerable.[19]

TENSIONS WITH INCREASED INTEREST IN NUCLEAR ENERGY

Nuclear energy currently provides about 15 percent of total global electricity. Its most ardent proponents have argued that the desire for diverse energy sources and nuclear power's benefits as a non-carbon-emitting energy source could lead to a doubling of current nuclear energy capacities by 2050.[20] Invoking a potential "nuclear renaissance," some countries have expressed reluctance, even hostility, toward efforts to strengthen international nonproliferation measures that might restrict their ambitions in the nuclear field in any way, particularly with respect to enrichment and reprocessing.

As an economic proposition, a nuclear renaissance of the kind envisioned by its most enthusiastic proponents is unlikely.[21] Nuclear reactors are costly to build, have an average project completion time of about a decade, require specialized materials and construction techniques, necessitate large numbers of qualified personnel, and do not now serve

many nonelectric transportation needs.[22] Safety and proliferation concerns also normally result in safety controls, regulatory regimes, international safeguards, and nuclear waste management. Those aspects of
nuclear energy present obstacles for countries that are planning either
new or major expansions of nuclear energy programs.[23]

For countries without extensive nuclear power–generating capabilities, there is currently little economic justification for enrichment
to produce reactor fuel. At present, domestic enrichment capability
begins to make economic sense only in nations with eight to ten operat-
ing nuclear power reactors.[24] (To put the intentions that lie behind Iran's
enrichment program in context, it has only one nuclear power reactor,
which is not yet fully operational, and a guaranteed supply of reactor
fuel from Russia.)[25] The commercial nuclear fuel market is diverse.
Six countries lead the international commercial enrichment market:
France, Germany, the Netherlands, Russia, the United Kingdom, and
the United States.[26] It makes little sense on purely economic grounds
for a nation to enter into the enrichment or reprocessing fields when it
can buy fuel from existing suppliers.[27]

Incorporating principles of economic viability into aspects of the
nonproliferation regime, such as requiring demonstrated economic
viability as a criterion for receiving any trade or transfer of sensitive
facilities, equipment, or technology, is thus one way to help prevent the
spread of dual-use capabilities such as enrichment and reprocessing to
countries with military or unclear intentions.

NONPROLIFERATION AND DISARMAMENT POLICIES: A COMPLEX RELATIONSHIP

Particularly in formal international settings, such as the quinquennial
NPT Review conferences, many nonnuclear weapon states have pro-
tested what they see as a lack of progress on arms control and disarmament by nuclear-armed states and have chafed at proposals to strengthen
nonproliferation measures. Some have cast the NPT obligations essentially as a set of ongoing tit-for-tat mini-bargains: nonproliferation rules
will be tightened if the nuclear weapon states, especially the United
States, pursue specific arms control and disarmament steps. Certain
proposals—to restrict the spread of enrichment and reprocessing, for

example—also meet with disapproval from some states that seek to block any limitations on rights, such as nuclear fuel production, that they claim have been granted by the NPT. Iran is prominent and vocal in this regard.

The politics of the nonproliferation regime need not and should not be so contentious. The NPT's origins, title, and text underscore that it is a treaty to prevent the spread of nuclear weapons. Article IV subordinates countries' rights regarding peaceful uses of nuclear energy to the nonproliferation provisions and purposes of the treaty. The framers of the NPT made a conscious decision not to enumerate the technologies to which nonnuclear weapon states had rights, and those unspecified rights were limited with reference to nonproliferation imperatives, not vice versa. Furthermore, the treaty states that the purpose of IAEA safeguards is "verification of the fulfillment of . . . obligations assumed under this Treaty with a view to preventing diversion of nuclear energy from peaceful uses to nuclear weapons or other nuclear explosive devices," implying that when safeguards cannot ensure that a state is adhering to its obligations, the safeguards must either be improved or the activities in question ceased.[28]

The long-term national interests of countries both with and without nuclear weapons favor strengthening the international nonproliferation regime. Proliferation of nuclear weapons, or of the ability to produce them quickly, particularly endangers nonnuclear weapon states. Those countries have no deterrent, other than an umbrella extended by existing nuclear weapon states, which in practice only the United States meaningfully provides. Preventing regional nuclear arms races requires significant bolstering of the international nonproliferation regime. The greatest danger to nuclear weapon states, and especially to nonnuclear weapon states, lies in the status quo: in leaving in place the existing nonproliferation rules and practices that are manifestly failing.

All states party to the NPT pledge to negotiate in good faith on measures related to cessation of the arms race and disarmament, and on a treaty for general and complete disarmament.[29] The United States and Russia have halted and reversed their nuclear arms race to a degree that would have astonished most of the framers of the NPT.[30] Since 1987, when President Ronald Reagan and Soviet general secretary Mikhail Gorbachev signed the Intermediate-Range Nuclear Forces Treaty, which abolished an entire category of nuclear weapons for the first time, the U.S. nuclear arsenal has plummeted to a level last known in the 1950s. The Obama administration is negotiating a new treaty with Russia to reduce levels further, expected to be signed in April 2010.

While the United States and Russia have been slashing their nuclear arsenals, others—notably China, which is a party to the NPT, and including India and Pakistan—are expanding theirs. Particularly troubling is the impact of the gradual but steady buildups in those countries on others in their regions, especially East Asia, which could lead to strategic recalculations of nuclear restraint by rivals and neighbors. U.S. secretary of defense Robert M. Gates's comments in January 2010 promoting the initiation of regular strategic nuclear talks with China are a useful first step, and an indication that China ought not receive a free pass on the destabilizing buildup of its nuclear forces.[31]

The argument that reducing the U.S. nuclear arsenal is itself a way to fight nuclear proliferation is difficult to sustain in light of the facts over the last two decades. As Mitchell Reiss has recently shown, "The size of our nuclear posture does not influence the motivations of potential proliferators. . . . the bottom line is that there is no positive correlation between the lowering of the U.S. and Russian nuclear arsenals and reducing nuclear proliferation around the world."[32] North Korea, Iran, and Syria have pursued nuclear programs with an actual or suspected military purpose while the United States has been cutting its arsenal dramatically. Nor have the deep reductions in the U.S. arsenal caused China, India, or Pakistan to cut their own.

The U.S. nuclear arsenal is qualitatively different from all others. Uniquely, it is, in critical respects, an instrument of nonproliferation. In important cases, countries that could easily develop nuclear weapons have refrained because of explicit or implicit protection afforded by the United States. At a minimum, the United States will have to consult closely with those countries as its arsenal drops further.[33]

Proliferation of weapons to states that have not previously possessed them will make further dramatic cuts in existing arsenals unlikely. Nuclear abolition—even among the eight longtime nuclear powers, between which relations, with the exception of India and Pakistan, are not currently antagonistic—is unfeasible without comprehensive solutions to regional and international security dilemmas and answers to verification problems. Disarmament becomes essentially impossible once other states—North Korea, potentially Iran, and perhaps others—develop nuclear arsenals, due to regional destabilization, weakening perceptions of the credibility of the U.S. nuclear umbrella, and failure of the nonproliferation regime to restrain proliferation. Too little attention has been given to how the choices made by new or latent nuclear weapon states affect the likelihood of reducing existing nuclear arsenals, particularly that of the United States.[34] At a time when the U.S. and Russian arsenals are plummeting, prioritizing disarmament over efforts to address the existing nonproliferation crises and shore up the nonproliferation regime may have perverse effects, as French president Nicolas Sarkozy recently emphasized at the UN Security Council.[35]

Recommendations

President Obama set out the contours of his disarmament and non-proliferation policy in speeches in Prague in April 2009 and to the UN Security Council in September 2009. He stated a commitment to pursue a world without nuclear weapons, with the caveats that the United States would maintain its nuclear arsenal as long as others did, and that nuclear abolition would not likely take place within his lifetime. He called for a follow-on Strategic Arms Reduction Treaty (START) with Russia by the end of 2009 and made clear that his administration would pursue Senate consent to the Comprehensive Test Ban Treaty (CTBT) and international negotiations for a Fissile Material Cutoff Treaty (FMCT).[36] He also said that he would strengthen international inspections, enforce nonproliferation obligations, and build a new framework for civil nuclear cooperation, including a fuel bank, though those nonproliferation goals were not set out in detail. To prevent nuclear terrorism or blackmail, the Obama administration has declared that it will seek to secure all vulnerable nuclear material within four years and is organizing an April 2010 nuclear security summit in Washington—putting nuclear security on the agenda of international leaders, emphasizing international cooperation, and spurring serious commitments and resources to the task.

The administration is pursuing each element of that approach on its perceived merits. Through its arms control and disarmament positions in particular (regarding the START follow-on treaty, CTBT, and FMCT), it concurrently seeks to remove arguments that some countries have put forth as diversionary and obfuscatory tactics, and to attempt to generate leverage with others to enlist their support for addressing nonproliferation challenges.

In September 2009, with President Obama presiding, the UN Security Council adopted Resolution 1887, which addressed arms control, disarmament, and nonproliferation.[37] The nonbinding resolution endorsed the main elements of the president's approach to arms control and disarmament. With respect to nonproliferation, the resolution emphasized the need for reforms, such as providing adequate detection authorities and capabilities for the IAEA, and tackling the problem of withdrawal from the NPT. It endorsed certain specific, helpful nonproliferation steps, including universal adherence to the Additional Protocol. For the most part, however, the resolution did not set out in detail measures to fortify the nonproliferation regime.

To date, President Obama's speeches and his administration's policy and actions have emphasized and been specific on arms control and disarmament policies but have been less explicit in setting forth detailed steps to strengthen the nonproliferation regime. The administration needs to shift focus and priorities toward binding measures to strengthen the nuclear nonproliferation regime.

USE POLITICAL CAPITAL FOR NONPROLIFERATION REGIME REFORM

The need for U.S. leadership and influence in the short term is great, and U.S. initiative will be essential to any successful effort to repair and bolster the regime. To date, the Obama administration's diplomatic strategy on the nonproliferation regime has been roundabout; it has attempted to use its positions on the CTBT, FMCT, and nuclear abolition to engender goodwill that will, in turn, be used to shore up the nonproliferation regime. A more direct diplomatic approach is necessary as well. The administration must forcefully make the case for specific meaningful and binding nonproliferation measures, emphasizing the extremely adverse security and economic consequences of continued proliferation. There is a broad strategic communications and education role for the U.S. government, and the president in particular, to set out clearly the danger to all states from proliferation, and to support initiatives to strengthen the regime—as well as to engage in direct, capital-to-capital diplomacy on the subject.

LIMIT THE EFFECTS OF THE NORTH KOREAN
AND IRANIAN NUCLEAR PROGRAMS

To limit North Korea and Iran from further damaging the nuclear non-proliferation regime, U.S. policy should be guided by two principles. First, preventing states from acquiring dangerous nuclear capabilities is easier and safer than trying to negotiate them out of those capabilities once they already possess them or after the development of those capabilities is under way. Preventing future nonproliferation crises requires tightening the rules and enforcement of the nonproliferation regime—which could apply to Iran, still a party to the NPT. Second, the models represented by the North Korean and Iranian nuclear programs to date must be made less attractive to nonnuclear weapon states than a continued policy of nuclear restraint. Even one rival appearing or starting to acquire nuclear weapons could begin to alter that calculus, as could a perception that nuclear blackmail of the kind practiced by North Korea produces net advantages. The Libya model—in which a country gives up its WMD programs and in turn is reintegrated into the international community—provides a precedent of an outcome that serves the country's ultimate interests and leads others to determine that pursuing WMD programs in the first place is unattractive. To increase the chances that Iran, North Korea, and others may follow something like the Libya model, and to discourage any other nation from pursuing their course thus far, requires raising the costs of their current actions.

With respect to Iran in particular, a considerable array of sanctions is still available, both U.S. and multilateral. At its own initiative, the U.S. Congress is considering imposing additional sanctions on Iran. The European Union (EU) decided in principle in late 2008 to apply new sanctions to Iran, though it backed off from formally adopting the sanctions. The United States should encourage the EU to apply those sanctions as a first step. It should also join with European and other like-minded countries to make clear to Iran that pressure on Tehran will increase rather than decrease, with steps clearly spelled out in advance, unless it ceases enrichment.

Economic sanctions can be used to increase the pressure on Iranian hardliners and to strengthen the hand of more moderate voices, and though existing sanctions are insufficient, they have had some effect. As a result of sanctions imposed between 2006 and 2008 by the UN

Security Council and by the United States acting unilaterally, most of the world's major banks and many large commercial actors have limited their dealing with Iran. The Department of the Treasury reports that "Iran's foreign borrowing has sharply declined since 2006" and "to the extent that Iranian firms have been able to replace lost credit with domestic credit, they are likely doing so at a much higher cost."[38] For an Iranian public already frustrated with their government's mismanagement of the economy, this creates an additional reason to side with opposition leaders, as Secretary Gates recently noted.[39]

The Obama administration has already highlighted the role of the Iranian Revolutionary Guard Corps' front companies, which dominate broad swaths of Iran's economy.[40] Additional sanctions could be used both to limit the resources available to the Iranian Revolutionary Guard Corps and to raise the costs for individual members by freezing their assets or prohibiting their travel. Sanctions could further restrict financial support for Iran's activities by preventing insurers from covering shipping companies or other front businesses known to be involved in illicit activities.

Although any sanctions would ideally be imposed through the UN Security Council and universally enforced, continued opposition by China to additional sanctions should not dissuade the United States and its allies from moving ahead in the absence of further Security Council action, and they should be prepared to pursue tough measures on top of Security Council steps if and when the council does act. The EU remains Iran's largest trading partner and can independently adopt sanctions that would impose significant trade and finance costs on the Iranian regime and the illicit businesses that support it. European sanctions would also have an important symbolic effect within the debate in Iran. A decision by Germany, which is Iran's main European trading partner, and Sweden and the Mediterranean countries, which are longstanding skeptics of sanctions, to support unilateral EU measures would send a public signal that the Iranian government is increasingly bringing about its isolation.

Financial sanctions are worth pursuing, not only because they can contribute to the broader diplomatic strategy on Iran, but also because they will send a powerful message to any other aspiring nuclear power that violating the nonproliferation regime will come at a considerable cost. Sanctions should be applied as part of a broader campaign of covert and political action against the Iranian regime.

RESTRICT THE SPREAD OF ENRICHMENT
AND REPROCESSING TECHNOLOGIES

Weaknesses in preventing the spread of enrichment and reprocessing, unless addressed, threaten to unravel the nonproliferation regime. The United States sought and maintained support within the Group of Eight (G8) for several years beginning in 2004 for a moratorium on trade in enrichment and reprocessing equipment and technology with countries that did not already possess full-scale, functioning plants for that purpose. It also sought to ensure that states without enrichment and reprocessing would have reliable, economic access to nuclear fuel. But the United States faced opposition in 2008, especially from nonnuclear weapon states—such as Canada—that possess natural uranium deposits and want to reserve the option to enrich as well as produce uranium.

The Obama administration should lead nuclear-supplying states in a global effort to adopt a criteria-based system to determine which countries could receive enrichment and reprocessing-related facilities, equipment, and technology from suppliers.[41] Since a moratorium is unsustainable, the next best option for restricting the spread of enrichment and reprocessing is to prevent their spread to those countries with military or unclear intentions. The question is not whether a line should be drawn, but where, and a criteria-based system regarding trade in sensitive nuclear technology would attempt to align intentions and capabilities in the nuclear field. The Bush administration proposed a criteria-based approach, drawing on an earlier French plan, to the NSG in 2008. It calls for suppliers not to authorize the transfer of enrichment and reprocessing facilities, equipment, and technology unless and until the recipient does the following:

– signs (and has in force) an Additional Protocol
– receives a clean bill of nonproliferation health from the IAEA
– adheres to NSG guidelines and implements effective export controls as required by UN Security Council Resolution 1540
– maintains an agreement with the supplier state that includes effective safeguards in perpetuity and retransfer provisions
– puts in place physical safety measures

The proposal also requires that countries receiving enrichment technology or information have national legislation prohibiting enrichment beyond low-enriched uranium. In addition, it calls on suppliers to consider other factors, such as whether the recipient has a credible and coherent rationale for pursuing enrichment or reprocessing in support of a civilian nuclear power reactor, and whether the transfer would harm the stability and security of the recipient and its region. It adds that suppliers should provide recipients with only "turnkey" or "black box" enrichment systems and facilities, limiting access to the underlying technology, and should consider participating in the operation of the facility.[42] Finally, the proposal provides that potential transferors should consult with other NSG members on the nonproliferation aspects of the transfer in advance.

The criteria-based proposal should be improved by making economic justification for enrichment or reprocessing one of the mandatory criteria, not simply a factor to be considered, and by requiring a detailed written report to NSG members laying out how each criterion, especially an economic justification, applies in any proposed case.

The criteria-based system would operate within the voluntary NSG. There are two ways to promote effective enforcement. First, each potential transferor should provide extensive information to the other NSG members in advance of each intended transfer. This step should be followed by extensive consultations with the other members, and, in questionable cases, presumptive favorable consideration to requests from other members that the potential transfer be called off. Second, restrictions on enrichment and reprocessing could be applied in as many different settings as possible. NSG members should agree that all bilateral nuclear cooperation agreements with states that do not currently possess fully functional enrichment or reprocessing plants should contain legally binding provisions that prohibit those states from enrichment and reprocessing. The recent U.S. agreement with the United Arab Emirates is a useful precedent.

The basic contours of the criteria-based proposal appear to have won support from virtually all countries within the NSG.[43] After signs in late 2008 that it might soon be adopted by the NSG, it stalled in mid-2009 when a few countries, including South Africa and Turkey, evidently raised issues with specific criteria.[44] In at least some of those cases, the issues seem to have been addressed. This relatively low-profile but meaningful reform, supported and encouraged by the Obama administration as it was by its predecessor, is an imminently achievable measure, perhaps as soon as the NSG plenary in June 2010. The Obama administration should emphasize it in high-level diplomacy to secure its final approval. Secretary of State Hillary Clinton's recent statement that the United States "will seek to strengthen Nuclear Suppliers Group restrictions on transfers of enrichment and reprocessing technology" is a hopeful indication that U.S. diplomacy to conclude a criteria-based system within the NSG may be pursued at high levels.[45] The adoption of a criteria-based proposal by the G8 in 2009 and positive references to conditional trade in sensitive nuclear technologies in Security Council Resolution 1887 should provide impetus for its prospects in the larger NSG.[46]

CLOSE GAPS IN EXISTING AGREEMENTS

The United States should pursue steps to restrict international transfers of sensitive nuclear equipment, technology, and materials in addition to those aimed narrowly at enrichment and reprocessing. Each of the steps below must be accomplished multilaterally to be effective.

The Obama administration should continue to press for universal signature, ratification, and implementation of the Additional Protocol, especially as a requirement for receiving any nuclear supply. The protocol, approved by the IAEA board of governors in 1997 to help detect clandestine nuclear programs, was developed in the wake of the discovery of the covert enrichment program in Saddam Hussein's Iraq. It requires expanded declarations of nuclear-related activities and provides the IAEA with increased access and environmental sampling rights, allowing the agency to compile a broader and more complete picture of a country's nuclear program and a greater chance to uncover covert activities.[47] Security Council Resolution 1887 encourages states to "consider" whether a recipient has ratified the Additional Protocol in making nuclear export decisions, a useful but nonbinding declaration. That condition should be applied in as many settings as possible, including in the NSG and in the final document of the NPT Review Conference. But the Additional Protocol is not a panacea. It does not provide inspectors with access to all possible nuclear facilities at all times.[48] And it should not be seen to excuse those who have adopted it from other nonproliferation obligations, including other inspections.

To further limit the spread of dangerous technologies, the United States should pursue two longer-term sets of measures at a lower priority. First, it should push for transparency in accounting for stockpiles of nuclear materials, with respect to weapons-usable material—the United States and some European countries already provide accounting of plutonium through the IAEA—and eventually all material.[49] Second, the United States should implement Title V of the Nuclear Nonproliferation Act of 1978, which requires analysis of countries' energy needs and how they can be met with nonfossil, nonnuclear energy sources.[50] Legislation has been introduced in both the Senate and the House to do so and should garner bipartisan support.[51]

PURSUE CONSTRUCTIVE MULTINATIONAL ALTERNATIVES TO NATIONAL PROGRAMS

The worthy objective of multilateral fuel supply proposals, several of which have been set out in recent years, is to create an alternative to national development of enrichment and reprocessing capabilities. The Obama administration, like the Bush administration, has favored such a system.[52] Yet there are reasons to proceed with caution. First, the existing commercial nuclear fuel market works: it is diverse, competitive, and reliable.[53] Any buyer of nuclear reactor fuel in today's market can acquire fuel from at least one supplier unless prohibited for proliferation reasons. Second, multinational supply arrangements alone will not achieve nonproliferation goals; they must be paired with restrictive arrangements by nuclear suppliers, as described above. Third, multinational approaches to fuel supply cannot solve proliferation challenges. At best, they can be a meaningful addition to the nonproliferation regime, which must be strengthened in its essential aspects.[54]

In all cases of multilateral fuel supply arrangements, such as an agreement by nuclear fuel suppliers to provide fuel to any buyer if existing supply is cut off for any reason other than proliferation concerns; a fuel bank under the auspices of the IAEA; or, less realistically, future multinational enrichment or reprocessing facilities, the following rules should be observed. Each fits under the rubric of "Do No

Harm." First, only countries with clean bills of health in nonproliferation, as determined by the IAEA and UN Security Council, should be
allowed to participate—and as many of the other criteria discussed
above, such as the Additional Protocol, should also apply if possible—
and those conditions should be ongoing requirements for continued
involvement.[55] Second, participating countries that do not have a fully
functional enrichment or reprocessing capability should make legally
binding commitments that include clear inspection and enforcement
provisions that they will not enrich or reprocess while participating
in the multilateral arrangement. Third, the arrangements should not
unduly subsidize or encourage the spread of nuclear technology.[56]

Multinational fuel production facilities are the least plausible of the
multilateral fuel supply arrangements commonly proposed. They are
also the riskiest, involving special challenges and dangers, and thus
would call for stricter ground rules. If such fuel production facilities
are pursued, the essential technology of the facilities should be black-
boxed: countries that do not currently possess the technologies in question should not have access to them, even if they have a financial and
managerial role in the arrangement.[57] Having all partners share in the
technology as well as in the financing and management of multinational
facilities would virtually ensure the ensuing spread of enrichment or
reprocessing covertly. The location of any multinational facility would
have to be selected carefully, perhaps applying at a minimum the criteria described above for recipients of enrichment technology. Multinational facilities are inherently vulnerable to nationalization; binding
rules for consequences in that event would need to be written into the
international agreement. A network of regional centers would raise the
location issue and increase opportunities for error. The history of existing multinational fuel production efforts has been one of changing and
ultimately incorrect assumptions about financing, the economic advantages of the arrangement, and the nature of the other governments that
participate—all reasons for caution in the future.

IMPROVE DETECTION OF NONCOMPLIANCE

The United States should direct efforts with other countries and
the leadership of the IAEA to ensure that the IAEA has the funding,
authority, technology, ability, and will to detect, determine, and report

noncompliance with safeguards obligations as effectively and quickly as possible. Those core tasks are critical to the viability of the nuclear nonproliferation regime and can be improved through specific steps. Though the Obama administration has emphasized the need for such measures, it has not spelled them out.[58]

The United States should press the IAEA to make full use of its existing authorities to request special inspections at undeclared sites and to obtain early design information on new nuclear facilities.[59] Denial of IAEA requests for either should be important factors in determining whether a state is complying with its obligations.

The Obama administration should continue to push for universal signature, ratification, and implementation of the Additional Protocol, which is in force in more than eighty states.[60] Yet the step is not a comprehensive fix, and it should not be seen as sufficient in addressing the IAEA's detection shortcomings. As former State Department official Mark Fitzpatrick has noted, the Additional Protocol "would help to provide transparency, but it is important to recognize the limitations of this verification measure. It does not provide for inspector access 'anytime, anywhere to all data, places and people,' and inspectors still would not be able to detect undeclared activity without prior information about the location of the facility."[61]

The United States should push for expanded inspection authorities for the IAEA. The IAEA should have near-real-time surveillance of potentially dangerous activities and materials—including fresh and spent reactor fuel—using cameras and sensors with secure feeds, which could help prevent diversion of those materials.[62] The United States should work with other countries to establish enhanced inspection authorities as standard requirements through multiple forums, such as the NSG, the NPT Review Conference, IAEA's board of governors, and bilateral nuclear cooperation agreements. For example, comprehensive authorization to access and inspect suspected nuclear-related areas, and real-time surveillance, should be made mandatory by the IAEA's board of governors and the UN Security Council in the event of serious questions from inspectors or the board of governors about a country's full compliance with safeguards obligations. The United States should also seek expanded power for the IAEA to require the disclosure of all trade, both export and import, in sensitive nuclear technology.[63]

The IAEA's resources have not kept abreast of its expanding safeguards responsibilities. It has depended in recent years on voluntary contributions from the United States and others. The IAEA's budget for inspections and technology should be expanded, and the IAEA should focus its resources on cases known or likely to pose proliferation challenges.

As a lower-priority measure, the United States should encourage the IAEA to revise counterproductive personnel policies, such as mandatory retirement ages, that may lead to unnecessary losses of expertise or prevent qualified and interested scientists and technical experts from joining the IAEA to help pursue its mission after previous careers.

As a long-term objective, the United States should encourage the IAEA to reassess its estimates and goals and present a more realistic picture of what can and cannot be considered safe.[64] One of the IAEA's principal objectives is to detect diversion of material from peaceful to military purposes with enough time before production of a weapon that the IAEA board of governors and UN Security Council can take effective action. The IAEA currently underestimates what constitutes a "significant quantity" of nuclear material—the "approximate amount of nuclear material for which the possibility of manufacturing a nuclear explosive device cannot be excluded"—and the IAEA's goals for timely detection can exceed the nuclear material's estimated conversion time.[65] The upshot is that the IAEA may not be able to detect a diversion in time. Senator Daniel Akaka (D-HI) has introduced a bill that would require the United States to undertake an assessment of the IAEA's capabilities—including the IAEA's ability to meet its timely detection inspection goals and whether the IAEA ought to revise its definitions of "significant quantity" and "conversion time"—and to work with the IAEA directly on those issues.[66] That legislation could provide a useful spur for action at the IAEA.

ESTABLISH AND FOLLOW GUIDELINES FOR DETERMINING NONCOMPLIANCE

The IAEA's board of governors must take a stricter view of a state's noncompliance with nonproliferation obligations. A one-time failure to report material or activities may indeed warrant a noncompliance finding. U.S. and Australian officials have in recent years suggested guidelines that should be issued publicly and used by the board, even if informally, in determining noncompliance.[67] The United States,

together with Australia and other interested countries, should propose
a set of guidelines and seek to introduce them into the IAEA board process. Among the guidelines should be that covert activities, especially
enrichment or reprocessing or steps toward them, or severe or system-
atic obstruction of IAEA investigations should almost always result in
a finding of noncompliance. The overall track record of the country on
nonproliferation, and evidence of both the intent and the capability of
the state to use the material, facilities, or technology for military purposes, should also weigh heavily in the determination. As a means for
making board determinations of noncompliance more fair, more objective, and more efficient, such guidelines may be welcomed by members
of the board.

STRENGTHEN ENFORCEMENT

The best way to address the enforcement challenges plaguing the nonproliferation regime today lies in a sequence of consecutively tougher
enforcement measures that are spelled out in advance (for deterrence
purposes) and triggered automatically if the violation is not remedied.
Secretary Clinton has stated that the United States "should consider
automatic penalties for violations of safeguards agreements, such as
suspending all IAEA technical cooperation until compliance has been
restored," but has not spelled out such an approach.[68] The United States
should push for adoption by the UN Security Council of a country-neutral, clearly stated sequence of enforcement steps that would apply to
states the IAEA board found to be in noncompliance (or against which
the Security Council otherwise decided to take action for proliferation-
related reasons) unless superseded by alternative Security Council
measures. China and Russia would be hard-pressed to justify vetoing
an objective, country-neutral approach—the adoption of which would
streamline enforcement and make it harder for countries to stall or
obstruct enforcement. Akin to criminal penalties set out in advance,
the defined and presumptively applicable measures would also serve to
deter violations of safeguards obligations in the first place.

Pierre Goldschmidt, the former IAEA deputy director general and
head of safeguards, has proposed a sensible plan that would address
many of the major concerns, the basic outline (but not all elements) of
which are included and recommended here.[69] The UN Security Council

should pass as soon as possible a resolution stating that it will pursue the following generic, country-neutral, presumptively applicable process for enforcement, unless it intervenes with a superseding resolution for tougher or less tough action in a particular case. First, after the board has found noncompliance and has requested expanded inspection authority, it would receive that expanded authority in an automatic but country-specific UN Security Council resolution that also applies punitive measures against the noncomplying state.[70] Second, if the board finds the country in continued noncompliance after a defined period, the Security Council would automatically pass resolutions on a set and expeditious timetable and with explicit terms, penalties, and consequences. It could start by requiring the country to suspend sensitive nuclear activities, eventually moving to international interdiction authority and cutting off nuclear, and then all military, trade to the country. Certain cases of noncompliance—for example, involving covert enrichment or reprocessing, or continual defiance of proscriptions—could proceed more quickly to the severest responses, such as stiff sanctions and cutting off nuclear trade.

Progressively graduated sanctions for breaking rules should allow flexibility for other avenues as necessary and for punitive measures to be stopped once the country in question demonstrates compliance with its safeguards and the resolutions. Should a particular case require an immediate and severe response, the UN Security Council could supersede its step-by-step approach with an intervening resolution.

ADDRESS WITHDRAWAL FROM THE NPT

As illustrated by North Korea's withdrawal from the NPT, the treaty's provision that allows for withdrawal after three months' notice poses significant challenges to the durability of the nuclear nonproliferation regime. Resolution 1887 noted the urgent need to address the withdrawal provision but did not provide details; it did helpfully lay down a marker by affirming "that a State remains responsible under international law for violations of the NPT committed prior to its withdrawal." Addressing the withdrawal provision is necessary to give the IAEA and UN Security Council time to act in the event of a notice to withdraw in a case where the country in question has been in violation of safeguards, and particularly where the country has exploited the NPT regime to develop or otherwise obtain dangerous technologies.

Amending the treaty to adjust the terms of Article X would be difficult. Instead, the United States could seek passage in the UN Security Council of a country-neutral, generic resolution stating that if a country gives notice of withdrawal from the treaty while in noncompliance with its obligations, as determined by the board or the UN Security Council, that country would face specific deterrent or punitive measures.[71] These could include intrusive inspections after the withdrawal and perhaps being considered a threat to international peace. It could also include mandatory dismantlement and the return of all nuclear equipment, technology, and material acquired while a member of the treaty upon request of the supplier, perhaps making the provision retroactive.[72]

Another possibility is to seek to lengthen the three-month period in which countries may withdraw from the NPT. That could be included in the NPT Review Conference final document in 2010, and then perhaps ensconced in an IAEA board of governors or UN Security Council resolution.

Conclusion

The international political context in which reforms must be advanced is contentious. Multilateral coordination and strict enforcement, especially by nuclear suppliers, are necessities, yet perceived national interests do not always overlap. Inherent in the nuclear nonproliferation regime are a divide between the "haves"—China, France, Russia, the United Kingdom, and the United States, the five states permitted under the NPT to possess nuclear weapons—and the "have-nots," the non-nuclear weapon states; an uneasy bargain involving nonproliferation, peaceful nuclear energy, and disarmament; and unclear or ineffective restrictions on dual-use technologies, such as enrichment and reprocessing, that can serve either civilian or military purposes, depending on the intentions of their possessor. Commercial interests can conflict with security objectives.

To be successful, proposals to strengthen the regime must be advanced with attention to the divergent postures of those involved. Some of the recommendations above have been set out in different form before. Yet the urgency of addressing the nonproliferation regime's flaws and renewed attention by international leaders to nuclear issues provide a basis for pursuing them vigorously now. The best approach is to advance reforms in a layered manner—that is, multilaterally and bilaterally, and, where possible, unilaterally—and across a range of forums, from the UN Security Council to the IAEA to less formal groups. A proposal may run into difficulties in one forum but be adopted in another, and building some overlap into the regime can help prevent a failure to adopt or enforce a rule in one setting from destabilizing the regime overall.

Endnotes

1. Enrichment is the process whereby the amount of the U-235 isotope in a quantity of uranium is increased from the level in which it is found in natural uranium, about 0.7 percent (the predominant isotope in natural uranium being U-238, at 99.3 percent). The complicated and costly process of enrichment—today done mostly by the centrifuge or gaseous diffusion methods, although laser enrichment projects are under way—can produce uranium in which U-235 comprises about 3 to 5 percent of the total. That is low-enriched uranium, or LEU, which can be used to fuel nuclear reactors. The same methods, however, can also bring the total percentage of the U-235 isotope in a quantity of uranium to much higher levels. Highly enriched uranium, or HEU—more than 20 percent U-235, preferably more than 90 percent—can be used as the fissile material in a nuclear weapon. By contrast to enrichment, reprocessing takes place at the "back end" of the nuclear fuel cycle, after spent fuel has been taken out of a nuclear reactor. Reprocessing is a chemical process (unlike enrichment, which is physical) that separates the plutonium, uranium, and fission products from each other in a spent fuel element. The plutonium is a potential reactor fuel, but it can also be used as the fissile material for a nuclear weapon.
2. Because of altered regional security dynamics caused by the North Korean and Iranian programs, or in pursuit of independently motivated nuclear ambitions (as in the case of Syria), additional countries could begin to climb the ladder of nuclear capabilities.
3. Article IV also states that all parties "undertake to facilitate, and have the right to participate in, the fullest possible exchange of equipment, materials and scientific and technological information for the peaceful uses of nuclear energy."
4. Article X requires that the three months' notice of withdrawal include an explanation of "extraordinary events, related to the subject matter of this Treaty" that the country judges to have "jeopardized its supreme interests."
5. Before the first Gulf War, Saddam Hussein's Iraq may have been only a year or eighteen months away from acquiring enough fissile material for a bomb. Theodore Hirsch, "The IAEA Additional Protocol: What It Is and Why It Matters," *The Nonproliferation Review*, Fall-Winter 2004, p. 142.
6. Wyn Bowen, "Libya," in James E. Doyle, ed., *Nuclear Safeguards, Security, and Nonproliferation: Achieving Security with Technology and Policy* (Butterworth-Heinemann, 2008), pp. 331–52.
7. Unless a state or nonstate actor can buy, steal, or otherwise acquire weapon-grade fissile material, enrichment or reprocessing is the most difficult and crucial aspect of producing a nuclear weapon.
8. North Korea tested nuclear devices in October 2006 and May 2009. Pyongyang recently stated that it is working to enrich uranium, the other principal method for making the fissile material for a nuclear weapon. "North Korea Claims Progress in Enriching Uranium," Reuters, September 3, 2009; Choe Sang-Hun, "N. Korea Issues

Threat on Uranium," *New York Times*, April 29, 2009. North Korea has not resolved suspicions that it already had, or has, a covert enrichment program. The bases for those suspicions include traces of highly enriched uranium found on documents turned over by North Korea that relate to its nuclear program. See Glenn Kessler, "New Data Found on North Korea's Nuclear Capacity," *Washington Post*, June 21, 2008, p. A08, and Hui Zhang, "Assessing North Korea's Uranium Enrichment Capabilities," *Bulletin of the Atomic Scientists*, June 18, 2009. North Korea is, moreover, a major proliferator of nuclear and missile technology to other regimes.

9. See undated U.S. government document, "Public Points for Qom Disclosure," http://www.politico.com/static/PPM41_public_points_for_qom_disclosure.html.

10. David Albright, Paul Brannan, and Jacqueline Shire, "IAEA Report on Iran," Institute for Science and International Security Report, August 28, 2009, p. 2; "Diplomats: Iran Has Means to Test Bombs in 6 Months," *Associated Press*, July 17, 2009. U.S. director of national intelligence Dennis C. Blair stated in February 2009 that Iran "probably would be technically capable of producing enough highly enriched uranium (HEU)" by 2010 at the earliest. Dennis C. Blair, "Annual Threat Assessment of the Intelligence Community for the Senate Select Committee on Intelligence," Unclassified Statement for the Record, February 12, 2009, p. 20. See also "Excerpts from Internal IAEA Document on Alleged Iranian Nuclear Weaponization," Institute for Science and International Security Report, October 2, 2009; William J. Broad and David E. Sanger, "Report Says Iran Has Data to Make a Nuclear Bomb," *New York Times*, October 4, 2009; "Iran could make an atom bomb, according to UN report's 'secret annexe,'" *Times of London Online*, October 5, 2009.

11. Mohammed ElBaradei quoted in Mark Landler, "Besieged Chief of Atomic Agency Carries On," *New York Times*, February 1, 2005; and in "Q&A: ElBaradei, Feeling the Nuclear Heat," *Washington Post*, January 30, 2005.

12. Robin Wright, "N. Koreans Taped at Syrian Reactor: Video Played Role in Israeli Raid," *Washington Post*, April 24, 2008.

13. Given the present ad hoc nature of enforcement, countries that have violated the rules have been able to count on certain supporters to block or dilute enforcement measures (while those supporters sometimes benefit politically and economically from the status quo). See, e.g., John Pomfret, "Oil, Ideology Keep China from Joining Push against Iran," *Washington Post*, September 30, 2009.

14. IAEA document GOV/2010/10, "Implementation of the NPT Safeguards Agreement and relevant provisions of Security Council resolutions 1737 (2006), 1747 (2007), 1803 (2008) and 1835 (2008) in the Islamic Republic of Iran," report by the Director General, February 18, 2010, pp. 8–10.

15. The IAEA is essential to the functioning of the international nuclear nonproliferation regime. Through bilateral agreements—for example, a comprehensive safeguards agreement and the Additional Protocol, which allows inspectors some expanded access to information and sites—with countries adhering to the NPT, the IAEA sets the terms of the safeguards that apply and verifies compliance with them. (Article III requires nonnuclear weapon states party to the treaty to accept safeguards in a separate agreement between the state and the IAEA.) The basic process by which the IAEA finds a country in noncompliance with its safeguards obligations starts with an IAEA inspectors' report of noncompliance. The inspectors' report is sent to the director general through the head of the Department of Safeguards. The director general sends the report to the board of governors; the board of governors formally determines noncompliance. At the same time as it finds noncompliance, or in sequence, the board calls upon the country in question to remedy the noncompliance and reports the noncompliance to the Security Council and members of the UN. See Pierre Goldschmidt,

Concrete Steps to Improve the Nonproliferation Regime, Carnegie Paper No. 100, Carnegie Endowment for International Peace, April 2009, p. 11. The IAEA board of governors has found noncompliance five times: Iraq (1991), Romania (1992), North Korea (1993), Libya (2004), and Iran (2006). John Carlson, "Defining Noncompliance: NPT Safeguards Agreements," *Arms Control Today*, vol. 39, no. 4, May 2009, p. 22.

16. National Intelligence Council, Office of the Director of National Intelligence, *Global Trends 2025: A World Transformed* (Washington, DC: November 2008), p. 62.

17. Ibid. See also Joseph Cirincione, *Bomb Scare: The History and Future of Nuclear Weapons* (New York: Columbia University Press, 2008), p. 172 (a "race has now begun among Arab countries to match Iran's nuclear capabilities"), and Bruce Riedel and Gary Samore, "Managing Nuclear Proliferation in the Middle East," in *Restoring the Balance: A Middle East Strategy for the Next President* (Washington, DC: Brookings Institution Press, 2008), p. 94 ("a nuclear Iran will prompt a regional nuclear arms race—indeed it already has begun"). As Thomas W. Lippman wrote about Saudi Arabia in 2004, before it expressed serious interest in pursuing nuclear energy: "Because energy, in the form of crude oil and natural gas, is the one resource Saudi Arabia possesses in abundance, no proposal for nuclear power would be credible." Lippmann, "Saudi Arabia: The Calculations of Uncertainty," in Kurt M. Campbell, Robert J. Einhorn, and Mitchell B. Reiss, eds., *The Nuclear Tipping Point: Why States Reconsider Their Nuclear Choices* (Washington, DC: Brookings Institution Press, 2004), p. 119. The same analysis applies to any number of countries in the Middle East now moving toward nuclear energy.

18. Riedel and Samore, "Managing Nuclear Proliferation in the Middle East," p. 94. There are unconfirmed reports that Saudi Arabia may have an opening to buy or otherwise acquire nuclear weapons from Pakistan. See Riedel and Samore, p. 117, and p. 129, footnote 15. See also Lippmann, "Saudi Arabia: The Calculations of Uncertainty," pp. 116, 121–22, 134–38.

19. NIC, *Global Trends 2025*, p. 62.

20. Sharon Squassoni, *Nuclear Energy: Rebirth or Resuscitation?* (Washington, DC: Carnegie Endowment for International Peace, 2009), p 1 Fossil fuels are required for the mining and enriching of uranium; the production of nuclear power is thus not carbon-emission free.

21. As Sharon Squassoni notes, "without major changes in government policies and aggressive financial support, nuclear power is actually likely to account for a *declining* percentage of global electricity generation." *Nuclear Energy*, p. 3 (emphasis in the original).

22. Charles D. Ferguson and Michelle M. Smith, "The Nuclear Option," *Foreign Policy*, January/February 2009, p. 40; Ferguson, *Nuclear Energy: Balancing Benefits and Risks*, Council Special Report No. 28 (New York: Council on Foreign Relations Press, April 2007), p. 15; *Nuclear Energy*, p. 7.

23. China, India, and Russia, among others, each have new reactors under construction and plans for more. No nuclear power reactors currently operate in the Middle East or Southeast Asia. Yet a number of countries in those regions—including Egypt, Saudi Arabia, the United Arab Emirates, Indonesia, and Vietnam—have plans, of varying degrees of sophistication, to acquire nuclear power. See U.S. Department of State International Security Advisory Board, *Report on Proliferation Implications of the Global Expansion of Civil Nuclear Power*, April 7, 2008; Ferguson and Smith, "The Nuclear Option," p. 40.

24. Ferguson, *Nuclear Energy*, p. 20. Mark Fitzpatrick puts the number at five to ten. Mark Fitzpatrick, *The Iranian Nuclear Crisis: Avoiding Worst-Case Outcomes*, Adelphi Paper No. 398 (London: International Institute for Strategic Studies/Routledge, 2008), p. 18.

25. Iran is also building a heavy-water reactor and associated facilities, ostensibly for re-
    search purposes. See IAEA document GOV/2010/10, "Implementation of the NPT
    Safeguards Agreement and relevant provisions of Security Council resolutions 1737
    (2006), 1747 (2007), 1803 (2008) and 1835 (2008) in the Islamic Republic of Iran," p. 5.
    If separated from the irradiated fuel, plutonium produced by those facilities could be
    used in a nuclear weapon.
26. Belgium, Italy, and Spain take part with France in a joint venture, Eurodif; its enrich-
    ment facility is located in France. Most of the enrichment market is led by four com-
    panies, including two international European consortiums. Brazil, China, and Japan
    have enrichment plants that largely or entirely service their own markets. France is
    the major international player in reprocessing spent nuclear fuel to recover plutonium
    commercially. India, Japan, Russia, and the United Kingdom have the capacity to re-
    process spent nuclear fuel to recover plutonium. Squassoni, *Nuclear Energy*, p. 51, fig.
    6, and p. 8, n. 13; Ferguson, *Nuclear Energy*, p. 16; IAEA, *Country Nuclear Fuel Cycle
    Profiles*, 2nd ed., 2005; World Nuclear Association.
27. Yet economics, diversification of energy supply, and combating climate change are not
    the only drivers behind some countries' interest in nuclear energy programs, and espe-
    cially in allowing leeway for enrichment and reprocessing. Perceived prestige, and the
    possibility of taking steps now to leave future nuclear options open, also loom large in
    some instances.
28. Article III.
29. Article VI.
30. One U.S. official wrote in a classified memo before U.S. ratification that Article VI is
    "an essentially hortatory statement." Memorandum from Spurgeon Keeny to Henry
    Kissinger, "Provisions of the NPT and Associated Problems," January 24, 1969.
31. Bill Gertz, "Gates wants nuclear talks with China," *Washington Times*, January 21, 2010.
32. Mitchell B. Reiss, "Confronting Global WMD Threats: New Direction of a New Ad-
    ministration, Implications for the U.S. Nuclear Posture of a Proliferated World: Now
    It Gets Complicated," conference paper, August 13–14, 2009, pp. 1–2.
33. It is thus possible that cuts to the quantity and composition of the U.S. nuclear arsenal
    could reach a point at which they unintentionally contribute to proliferation.
34. As UN General Assembly Resolution 1665, which helped guide the NPT negotiations,
    stated, "an increase in the number of States possessing nuclear weapons is growing
    more imminent and threatens to extend and intensify the arms race and to increase
    the difficulties of avoiding war and establishing peace and security based on the rule
    of law." Mitchell Reiss notes that nuclear proliferation will likely generate pressure on
    the United States to increase its nuclear arsenal: "The United States will be tempted to
    extend security assurances and guarantees to cope with two new nuclear-armed states
    and to try to prevent North Korea and Iran from triggering a cascade of additional
    nuclear proliferation in their respective regions." Reiss, "Confronting Global WMD
    Threats: New Direction of a New Administration," p. 4; see also pp. 3, 6–8.
35. "We are right to speak of the future, but before the future there is the present, and at
    present we have two nuclear crises. The people of the entire world are listening to what
    we are saying, to our promises, our commitments and our speeches, but we live in a
    real world, not a virtual world. . . . If we want in the end to have a world without nuclear
    weapons, let us not accept the violation of international rules." Speech by Nicolas Sar-
    kozy to the UN Security Council, Summit on Nuclear Non-Proliferation, September
    24, 2009.
36. Two U.S. presidents have favored and sought the near-term abolition of nuclear weap-
    ons. The first was Harry Truman, who proposed the Baruch Plan to abolish nuclear
    weapons and internationalize nuclear energy, at a time when the United States had

a monopoly on the atomic bomb. Ronald Reagan was the other. See S. David Bro-scious, "Longing for International Control, Banking on American Superiority: Harry S. Truman's Approach to Nuclear Weapons," in John Lewis Gaddis, Philip H. Gordon, Ernest R. May, and Jonathan Rosenberg, eds., *Cold War Statesmen Confront the Bomb: Nuclear Diplomacy since 1945* (Oxford: Oxford University Press, 1999), and Paul Lettow, *Ronald Reagan and His Quest to Abolish Nuclear Weapons* (New York: Random House, 2005).

37. S.C. Res. 1887 (September 24, 2009).
38. Written testimony by Under Secretary of the Treasury for Terrorism and Financial Intelligence Stuart Levey before the Senate Committee on Banking, Housing, and Urban Affairs, "Minimizing Potential Threats from Iran: Administration Perspectives on Economic Sanctions and Other United States Policy Options," October 6, 2009, http://www.ustreas.gov/press/releases/tg314.htm.
39. As Secretary Gates recently stated, "It's clear in the aftermath of the election that there are some fairly deep fissures in Iranian society and politics and—and probably even in the leadership. . . . this is one of the reasons why I think additional and espe-cially severe economic sanctions could have some real impact. . . . we know that the sanctions that have already been placed on the country have had an impact." Inter-view of Robert Gates by John King, CNN, September 27, 2009, http://157.166.255.31/ TRANSCRIPTS/0909/27/sotu.01.html.
40. "Treasury Targets Iran's Islamic Revolutionary Guard Corps," February 10, 2010, http://www.treas.gov/press/ releases/tg539.htm.
41. A criteria-based proposal is consistent with Article IV of the NPT. It would aim to ensure that any enrichment and reprocessing transfers that occur do not further a country's nuclear weapon ambitions—and thus that the recipient pursues its peaceful nuclear energy "in conformity with articles I and II" of the NPT, as required by Article IV. Iran would fail to qualify under the terms of the criteria precisely because its nu-clear efforts cannot be demonstrated to be peaceful in nature. Yet that raises a warning about the intersection of a criteria-based system and nuclear negotiations with Iran. Iran does not meet the criteria and is unlikely to in the foreseeable future; if it were allowed to continue enrichment under the terms of a negotiated deal, whereas other countries (for example, Australia and Canada) must meet the criteria to receive enrich-ment and reprocessing trade from suppliers, it would undermine the credibility of the system, and Iran would essentially have been rewarded for pursuing and expanding a covert enrichment program even as the UN Security Council mandated that it stop. The United States and others may end up accepting that inconsistency if its benefits override its detriments. If accepted, it would have to be offset by unique and exception-ally strict trade, inspection, and enforcement provisions.
42. Miles A. Pomper, "Nuclear Suppliers Make Progress on New Rules," *Arms Control Today*, vol. 38, no. 10 (December 2008), p. 52. The black box provision of the criteria makes sense from an economic and nonproliferation standpoint. It is accepted today—on the recipient side—by states that possess both nuclear weapons and enrichment capability. France and the United States have agreed in recent years to receive enrich-ment technology from a centrifuge company associated with URENCO only in "black box," such that French and U.S. personnel will not have access to the enrichment tech-nology. See National Academy of Sciences, National Research Council, and Russian Academy of Sciences, *Internationalization of the Nuclear Fuel Cycle: Goals, Strategies, and Challenges* (Washington, DC: National Academies Press, 2008), p. 25.
43. Daniel Horner, "Accord on New Rules Eludes Nuclear Suppliers," *Arms Control Today*, vol. 39, no. 6 (July/August 2009), pp. 29–30.
44. Ibid.

45. Hillary Rodham Clinton, "The Next Steps on Nonproliferation," *Foreign Policy*, October 28, 2009.

46. G8, "L'Aquila Statement on Non-Proliferation," July 2009; Daniel Horner, "G-8 Tightens Nuclear Export Rules," *Arms Control Today*, vol. 39, no. 7 (September 2009), pp. 33–34; and S.C. Res. 1887 (September 24, 2009).

47. Hirsch, "The IAEA Additional Protocol: What It Is and Why It Matters," pp. 143–52, 159.

48. Ibid., p. 143.

49. George Perkovich et al., *Universal Compliance: A Strategy for Nuclear Security* (Washington, DC: Carnegie Endowment for International Peace, 2007), pp. 108–09.

50. *World at Risk: The Report of the Commission on the Prevention of WMD Proliferation and Terrorism* (New York: Vintage Books, 2008), p. 51; Henry D. Sokolski, "Market-Fortified Nonproliferation," in Jeffrey Laurenti and Carl Robichaud, eds., *Breaking the Nuclear Impasse: New Prospects for Security against Weapons Threats* (New York: The Century Foundation Press, 2007), pp. 88–89; and Henry Sokolski, "Avoiding a Nuclear Crowd," *Policy Review*, June/July 2009, no. 155, pp. 30–32.

51. S. 1675, "Energy Development Program Implementation Act," September 16, 2009.

52. Clinton, "The Next Steps on Nonproliferation," *Foreign Policy*, October 28, 2009.

53. As the international expert group convened by then-IAEA director general ElBaradei to explore multilateral approaches to the nuclear fuel cycle stated, "the legitimate objective of assurances of supply can be fulfilled to a large extent by the market." IAEA Information Circular (INFCIRC)/640, "Multilateral Approaches to the Nuclear Fuel Cycle: Expert Group Report Submitted to the Director General of the International Atomic Energy Agency," February 22, 2005, p. 6; see also p. 30. The National Academy of Sciences and Russian Academy of Sciences concur: "The existing international market provides strong assurance of supply." National Academy of Sciences et al., *Internationalization of the Nuclear Fuel Cycle*, p. 3.

54. "The primary technical barriers against proliferation remain the effective and universal implementation of IAEA safeguards under comprehensive safeguards agreements and additional protocols, and export controls. Both must be as strong as possible in their own merits. MNAs [multilateral nuclear approaches] will be complementary mechanisms for strengthening the regime." IAEA INFCIRC/640, "Multilateral Approaches to the Nuclear Fuel Cycle," p. 98.

55. The conditions and criteria could be adjusted to bring a country like Iran into a multilateral arrangement as part of an agreement that verifiably ended its enrichment program.

56. Among the possibilities that would actually further the spread of dangerous technologies is that, as Charles Ferguson has pointed out, "a country could take advantage of a fuel assurance initiative to launch a nuclear power program, reasoning that buying fuel is initially cheaper than making its own fuel," which it would not have done to begin with. Ferguson, *Nuclear Energy*, p. 20. After building a significant number of reactors, it could withdraw from the multinational arrangement and develop its own enrichment or reprocessing capabilities. There are few ways to overcome this problem, other than the probably unrealistic solution of including binding terms in an initial agreement that even after a country has withdrawn from a multinational arrangement, it will not pursue enrichment or reprocessing for a certain period. See also *World at Risk*, in which the bipartisan Commission on the Prevention of WMD Proliferation and Terrorism discourages, "to the extent possible, the subsidizing of nuclear energy in ways that would cause states to choose it over other energy sources, without fully accounting for this risk," p. 56, and recommends ensuring access to nuclear fuels at market

prices for "nonnuclear states that agree not to develop sensitive fuel cycle capabilities and are in full compliance with international obligations," p. 47.

57. There is precedent for this: France and the United States have agreed to deals that black box centrifuge technology associated with URENCO; in the French-led Eurodif consortium, technology based only in France produces fuel supplied to the partners. National Academy of Sciences et al., *Internationalization of the Nuclear Fuel Cycle*, p. 25.

58. Secretary Clinton has stated that the United States "supports enhancing the IAEA's verification authorities and resources so that it can perform its mission effectively." Clinton, "The Next Steps on Nonproliferation," *Foreign Policy*, October 28, 2009.

59. Goldschmidt, *Concrete Steps to Improve the Nonproliferation Regime*, pp. 5–9.

60. UN Security Resolution 1887, passed in September 2009, helpfully "*calls upon* all States to sign, ratify and implement an additional protocol, which together with comprehensive safeguards agreements constitute essential elements of the IAEA safeguards system" (emphasis in original).

61. Fitzpatrick, "The Iranian Nuclear Crisis," p. 22. See also Hirsch, "The IAEA Additional Protocol: What It Is and Why It Matters," pp. 140–166.

62. Henry D. Sokolski, "Assessing the IAEA's Ability to Verify the NPT," in Henry D. Sokolski, ed., *Falling Behind: International Scrutiny of the Peaceful Atom* (Carlisle, PA: Strategic Studies Institute, 2008), p. 22.

63. Goldschmidt, *Concrete Steps to Improve the Nonproliferation Regime*, pp. 10–11.

64. Sokolski, "Assessing the IAEA's Ability," pp. 7–10; Thomas B. Cochran, "Adequacy of IAEA's Safeguards for Achieving Timely Detection," pp. 121–57, both in Sokolski, *Falling Behind*.

65. Cochran, "Adequacy of IAEA's Safeguards," pp. 123, 151.

66. S. 1931, "Strengthening the Oversight of Nuclear Nonproliferation Act of 2009," October 27, 2009.

67. The State Department proposes that considerations "relevant in assessing the significance of a safeguards problem include: the nature and quantity of the material involved; the relevance of the activity in question to nuclear weapons development (e.g., enrichment or reprocessing versus civil nuclear reactor operations); and the degree to which the problem is part of a pattern of similar or related problems." U.S. Department of State, *Adherence to and Compliance with Arms Control, Nonproliferation and Disarmament Agreements and Commitments*, August 2005, pp. 67–69. I thank Christopher Ford, who played a key role in the U.S. proposal, for the reference. See also Carlson, "Defining Noncompliance," pp. 22–26; Goldschmidt, *Concrete Steps to Improve the Nonproliferation Regime*, pp. 11–12.

68. Clinton, "The Next Steps on Nonproliferation," *Foreign Policy*, October 28, 2009.

69. Goldschmidt, *Concrete Steps to Improve the Nonproliferation Regime*, pp. 12–16.

70. The Security Council would reserve the right to take action in cases even without prior board determination of noncompliance.

71. Goldschmidt, *Concrete Steps to Improve the Nonproliferation Regime*, pp. 15–16.

72. As with the enforcement recommendations, the proposed withdrawal resolution would aim at least as much to deter as to be brought into action, and could be applicable to Iran.

About the Author

Paul Lettow is an adjunct senior fellow for national security studies at the Council on Foreign Relations. He served as the senior director for strategic planning and institutional reform on the National Security Council staff from 2007 to 2009, and as a senior adviser to the under-secretary of state for democracy and global affairs from 2006 to 2007. Lettow is the author of *Ronald Reagan and His Quest to Abolish Nuclear Weapons*. He was a law clerk to Chief Judge Danny J. Boggs of the U.S. Court of Appeals for the Sixth Circuit. He received an AB in history from Princeton University, a JD from Harvard Law School, and a DPhil in international relations from Oxford University.

Advisory Committee for *Strengthening the Nuclear Nonproliferation Regime*

J. Michael Allen III
Bipartisan Policy Center

John P. Barker
Arnold & Porter LLP

Gary K. Bertsch
University of Georgia

Charles D. Ferguson II, *ex officio*
Council on Foreign Relations

Christopher A. Ford
Hudson Institute

Stephen J. Hadley
U.S. Institute of Peace

Alan Hanson
AREVA Inc.

Thomas D. Lehrman
Boliven LLC

Michael A. Levi, *ex officio*
Council on Foreign Relations

Thomas G. Mahnken
*Paul H. Nitze School of Advanced
International Studies*

Stewart M. Patrick, *ex officio*
Council on Foreign Relations

Gabriel B. Pellathy
Westinghouse Electric Corp.

Stephen G. Rademaker
BGR Holding LLC

Charles S. Robb
George Mason University

Andrew K. Semmel
AKS Consulting

Henry D. Sokolski
Nonproliferation Policy Education Center

Jasper A. Welch Jr.
SAIC Strategies Group

Mission Statement of the International Institutions and Global Governance Program

The International Institutions and Global Governance (IIGG) program at CFR aims to identify the institutional requirements for effective multilateral cooperation in the twenty-first century. The program is motivated by recognition that the architecture of global governance—largely reflecting the world as it existed in 1945—has not kept pace with fundamental changes in the international system. These shifts include the spread of transnational challenges, the rise of new powers, and the mounting influence of nonstate actors. Existing multilateral arrangements thus provide an inadequate foundation for addressing many of today's most pressing threats and opportunities and for advancing U.S. national and broader global interests.

Given these trends, U.S. policymakers and other interested actors require rigorous, independent analysis of current structures of multilateral cooperation, and of the promises and pitfalls of alternative institutional arrangements. The IIGG program meets these needs by analyzing the strengths and weaknesses of existing multilateral institutions and proposing reforms tailored to new international circumstances.

The IIGG program fulfills its mandate by

- Engaging CFR fellows in research on improving existing and building new frameworks to address specific global challenges—including climate change, the proliferation of weapons of mass destruction, transnational terrorism, and global health—and disseminating the research through books, articles, Council Special Reports, and other outlets;

- Bringing together influential foreign policymakers, scholars, and CFR members to debate the merits of international regimes and frameworks at meetings in New York, Washington, DC, and other select cities;

- Hosting roundtable series whose objectives are to inform the foreign policy community of today's international governance challenges and breed inventive solutions to strengthen the world's multilateral bodies; and

- Providing a state-of-the-art Web presence as a resource to the wider foreign policy community on issues related to the future of global governance.

Council Special Reports

Published by the Council on Foreign Relations

Preparing for Sudden Change in North Korea
Paul B. Stares and Joel S. Wit; CSR No. 42, January 2009
A Center for Preventive Action Report

Averting Crisis in Ukraine
Steven Pifer; CSR No. 41, January 2009
A Center for Preventive Action Report

Congo: Securing Peace, Sustaining Progress
Anthony W. Gambino; CSR No. 40, October 2008
A Center for Preventive Action Report

Deterring State Sponsorship of Nuclear Terrorism
Michael A. Levi; CSR No. 39, September 2008

China, Space Weapons, and U.S. Security
Bruce W. MacDonald; CSR No. 38, September 2008

Sovereign Wealth and Sovereign Power: The Strategic Consequences of American Indebtedness
Brad W. Setser; CSR No. 37, September 2008
A Maurice R. Greenberg Center for Geoeconomic Studies Report

Securing Pakistan's Tribal Belt
Daniel Markey; CSR No. 36, July 2008 (Web-only release) and August 2008
A Center for Preventive Action Report

Avoiding Transfers to Torture
Ashley S. Deeks; CSR No. 35, June 2008

Global FDI Policy: Correcting a Protectionist Drift
David M. Marchick and Matthew J. Slaughter; CSR No. 34, June 2008
A Maurice R. Greenberg Center for Geoeconomic Studies Report

Dealing with Damascus: Seeking a Greater Return on U.S.-Syria Relations
Mona Yacoubian and Scott Lasensky; CSR No. 33, June 2008
A Center for Preventive Action Report

Climate Change and National Security: An Agenda for Action
Joshua W. Busby; CSR No. 32, November 2007
A Maurice R. Greenberg Center for Geoeconomic Studies Report

Planning for Post-Mugabe Zimbabwe
Michelle D. Gavin; CSR No. 31, October 2007
A Center for Preventive Action Report

The Case for Wage Insurance
Robert J. LaLonde; CSR No. 30, September 2007
A Maurice R. Greenberg Center for Geoeconomic Studies Report

Reform of the International Monetary Fund
Peter B. Kenen; CSR No. 29, May 2007
A Maurice R. Greenberg Center for Geoeconomic Studies Report

Nuclear Energy: Balancing Benefits and Risks
Charles D. Ferguson; CSR No. 28, April 2007

Nigeria: Elections and Continuing Challenges
Robert I. Rotberg; CSR No. 27, April 2007
A Center for Preventive Action Report

The Economic Logic of Illegal Immigration
Gordon H. Hanson; CSR No. 26, April 2007
A Maurice R. Greenberg Center for Geoeconomic Studies Report

The United States and the WTO Dispute Settlement System
Robert Z. Lawrence; CSR No. 25, March 2007
A Maurice R. Greenberg Center for Geoeconomic Studies Report

Bolivia on the Brink
Eduardo A. Gamarra; CSR No. 24, February 2007
A Center for Preventive Action Report

After the Surge: The Case for U.S. Military Disengagement from Iraq
Steven N. Simon; CSR No. 23, February 2007

Darfur and Beyond: What Is Needed to Prevent Mass Atrocities
Lee Feinstein; CSR No. 22, January 2007

Avoiding Conflict in the Horn of Africa: U.S. Policy Toward Ethiopia and Eritrea
Terrence Lyons; CSR No. 21, December 2006
A Center for Preventive Action Report

Living with Hugo: U.S. Policy Toward Hugo Chávez's Venezuela
Richard Lapper; CSR No. 20, November 2006
A Center for Preventive Action Report

Reforming U.S. Patent Policy: Getting the Incentives Right
Keith E. Maskus; CSR No. 19, November 2006
A Maurice R. Greenberg Center for Geoeconomic Studies Report

Foreign Investment and National Security: Getting the Balance Right
Alan P. Larson and David M. Marchick; CSR No. 18, July 2006
A Maurice R. Greenberg Center for Geoeconomic Studies Report

Challenges for a Postelection Mexico: Issues for U.S. Policy
Pamela K. Starr; CSR No. 17, June 2006 (Web-only release) and November 2006

U.S.-India Nuclear Cooperation: A Strategy for Moving Forward
Michael A. Levi and Charles D. Ferguson; CSR No. 16, June 2006

Generating Momentum for a New Era in U.S.-Turkey Relations
Steven A. Cook and Elizabeth Sherwood-Randall; CSR No. 15, June 2006

Peace in Papua: Widening a Window of Opportunity
Blair A. King; CSR No. 14, March 2006
A Center for Preventive Action Report

Neglected Defense: Mobilizing the Private Sector to Support Homeland Security
Stephen E. Flynn and Daniel B. Prieto; CSR No. 13, March 2006

Afghanistan's Uncertain Transition From Turmoil to Normalcy
Barnett R. Rubin; CSR No. 12, March 2006
A Center for Preventive Action Report

Preventing Catastrophic Nuclear Terrorism
Charles D. Ferguson; CSR No. 11, March 2006

Getting Serious About the Twin Deficits
Menzie D. Chinn; CSR No. 10, September 2005
A Maurice R. Greenberg Center for Geoeconomic Studies Report

Both Sides of the Aisle: A Call for Bipartisan Foreign Policy
Nancy E. Roman; CSR No. 9, September 2005

Forgotten Intervention? What the United States Needs to Do in the Western Balkans
Amelia Branczik and William L. Nash; CSR No. 8, June 2005
A Center for Preventive Action Report

A New Beginning: Strategies for a More Fruitful Dialogue with the Muslim World
Craig Charney and Nicole Yakatan; CSR No. 7, May 2005

Power-Sharing in Iraq
David L. Phillips; CSR No. 6, April 2005
A Center for Preventive Action Report

*Giving Meaning to "Never Again": Seeking an Effective Response to the Crisis
in Darfur and Beyond*
Cheryl O. Igiri and Princeton N. Lyman; CSR No. 5, September 2004

Freedom, Prosperity, and Security: The G8 Partnership with Africa: Sea Island 2004 and Beyond
J. Brian Atwood, Robert S. Browne, and Princeton N. Lyman; CSR No. 4, May 2004

Addressing the HIV/AIDS Pandemic: A U.S. Global AIDS Strategy for the Long Term
Daniel M. Fox and Princeton N. Lyman; CSR No. 3, May 2004
Cosponsored with the Milbank Memorial Fund

Challenges for a Post-Election Philippines
Catharin E. Dalpino; CSR No. 2, May 2004
A Center for Preventive Action Report

Stability, Security, and Sovereignty in the Republic of Georgia
David L. Phillips; CSR No. 1, January 2004
A Center for Preventive Action Report

Note: Council Special Reports are available for download from CFR's website, www.cfr.org.
For more information, email publications@cfr.org.

www.ingramcontent.com/pod-product-compliance
Lightning Source LLC
Chambersburg PA
CBHW060522280326
41933CB00014B/3073